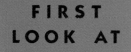

FIRST LOOK AT

RIVERS

For a free color catalog describing Gareth Stevens' list of high-quality children's books, call 1-800-341-3569 (USA) or 1-800-461-9120 (Canada).

Library of Congress Cataloging-in-Publication Data

Baker, Susan, 1961-
    First look at rivers / Susan Baker.
      p. cm. — (First look)
    "North American edition"—T.p. verso.
    Includes bibliographical references and index.
    Summary: Explains how rivers begin, travel, and end, and how they benefit humankind.
    ISBN 0-8368-0679-4
    1. Rivers—Juvenile literature. [1. Rivers.] I. Title. II. Series.
GB1203.8.B35 1991
551.48′3—dc20
                                                 91-9419

North American edition first published in 1991 by

Gareth Stevens Children's Books
1555 North RiverCenter Drive, Suite 201
Milwaukee, Wisconsin 53212, USA

U.S. edition copyright © 1991 by Gareth Stevens, Inc. First published as *Rivers* in the United Kingdom, copyright © 1991, by Simon & Schuster Young Books. Additional end matter copyright © 1991 by Gareth Stevens, Inc.

Photograph credits: Bruce Coleman, 7, 8, 9; Robert Harding, 24; ZEFA, all others

Series editor: Patricia Lantier-Sampon
Design: M&M Design Partnership
Cover design: Laurie Shock
Layout: Sharone Burris

Printed in the United States of America

1 2 3 4 5 6 7 8 9 97 96 95 94 93 92 91

15719

FIRST LOOK AT

RIVERS

SUSAN BAKER

Gareth Stevens Children's Books
MILWAUKEE

Books in the
FIRST LOOK series:

FIRST LOOK AT
THE AIRPORT

FIRST LOOK AT
BOATS

FIRST LOOK AT
CARS

FIRST LOOK AT
CHANGING SEASONS

FIRST LOOK AT
CLOTHES

FIRST LOOK AT
DAY AND NIGHT

FIRST LOOK IN
THE FOREST

FIRST LOOK AT
GROWING FOOD

FIRST LOOK IN
THE HOSPITAL

FIRST LOOK
IN THE AIR

FIRST LOOK AT
KEEPING WARM

FIRST LOOK AT
MOUNTAINS

FIRST LOOK AT
RIVERS

FIRST LOOK
UNDER THE GROUND

FIRST LOOK
UNDER THE SEA

FIRST LOOK AT
USING ENERGY

CONTENTS

Down by the River 6

Where Does a River Come From? 8

Valleys and Waterfalls 10

Flowing to the Sea 12

Is There a River Nearby? 14

River Wildlife 16

Fishing 18

Farming by Rivers 20

Rivers at Work 22

Crossing Places 24

Living by Rivers 26

Bridges 28

More Books about Rivers 30

Glossary 30

Index 32

DOWN BY THE RIVER

Ducks swim close to the bank, looking for food. A motorboat is tied up at the dock, ready for its next trip.

What do you like to do by the river?

Have you ever stood on a bridge over a river and watched the water flowing underneath? Which way does it go?

7

WHERE DOES A RIVER COME FROM?

After a rainfall, water flows down the hillsides, soaking into the soil and trickling over the stones.

The water meets and joins other streams. Together they make a river. Have you ever seen a river at its source?

VALLEYS AND WATERFALLS

Torrents of water tumble downhill, sweeping mud and rocks along.

Water makes its way around hard rock and through soft places. If it meets a hard ledge, it tumbles over and makes a waterfall.

Water grinds the rock away as it flows, cutting deep valleys and gorges.

Have you ever seen a waterfall? What kind of sound did it make?

11

FLOWING TO THE SEA

In flat countryside, rivers glide calmly along.
Plants and trees grow along the banks.

Rivers flow slowly across plains. Where does
a river end?

14

IS THERE A RIVER NEARBY?

Is the water clean and clear? What can you find there?

In some rivers the water is dirty. Fish die, and small channels are blocked with garbage and mud.

Why must we try to keep our rivers free from pollution? How can we do this?

RIVER WILDLIFE

Watch the insects moving above, in, and on the water. The dragonfly is the biggest of all.

Have you ever collected frog eggs? What happens to them after a while?

It's fun to look for fish in a river. Kingfishers and otters catch fish to eat.

17

18

FISHING

People fish from riverbanks, bridges, and boats. What do people use to catch fish? Have you tried using a net or a pole?

When you are near a river, you must be careful not to fall in.

FARMING BY RIVERS

Animals graze beside the river and drink its water.

When a river floods, it covers the valley floor with a thick layer of mud. Crops grow well in this rich soil.

21

RIVERS AT WORK

People use rivers and waterpower to help them with their work.

Water turns the wheel at the mill.

Huge, heavy barges chug steadily up and down the river. What do barges carry?

CROSSING PLACES

Rivers sometimes cross the path of people who are traveling. How are these hikers getting across?

Ferryboats take people across deep, wide rivers. What else can ferryboats carry?

LIVING BY RIVERS

What do people need water for? Farms and villages were built near rivers long ago. Some villages have grown into cities.

Rivers used to be important highways. How do people usually travel now?

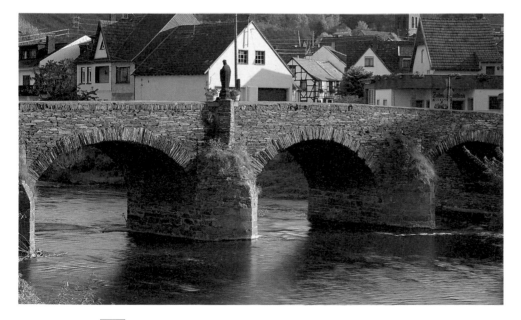

27

BRIDGES

Bridges are roads that allow people to cross a river. Cars, trucks, and trains can cross a river on bridges, too.

What are bridges made of?

Is there a river near your home? What kind of bridge do you use to cross it?

Is the river wide?

29

More Books about Rivers

A Day on the River. Michl (Barron's Educational Series)
In the Water . . . On the Water. Chlad (Childrens Press)
Our Changing World: The River. Bellamy (Crown Publishers)
Rivers. N. Carlisle and M. Carlisle (Childrens Press)
Splash and Trickle. Green (Rainbow Books)
Water. Webb (Franklin Watts)
Water: What It Is, What It Does. Seixas (Greenwillow Books)
The Water Book: Where It Came from and Where It Goes. Freeman and Morrison
    (Random House)
Water is Wet. Pollock (Putnam Publishing Group)
The Wind in the Willows. Grahame (Macmillan)
Wonders of Rivers. Bains (Troll Associates)

Glossary

Bank: A long piece of land that stretches along the side of a body of water. Different kinds of plants and trees usually grow along the banks of a river or stream.

Barge: A large boat with a flat bottom that is used to haul huge loads of supplies or other materials on a body of water.

Dock: A place where boats can be put into the water. Docks are also places where boats can land and stay safely tied until the next fishing or boating trip.

Ferryboat: A special boat used to carry people, cars, buses, trains, and different products across a body of water.

Gorge: A deep, narrow passageway between tall mountains, hills, or cliffs.

Graze: To eat grass that grows in a field or other open area. Cows and sheep are examples of animals that graze.

Kingfisher: A brightly colored bird with a strong beak. Kingfishers hunt for fish in rivers and streams.

Mill: A building or group of buildings with special machines that grind grain or some other crop so that people can use it for some purpose. A mill can also be any type of factory that makes a special product.

Otter: A water animal with webbed feet and a long, flat tail. Otters like to catch and eat fish.

Pollute: To make something dirty. Many rivers are now polluted because people have dumped garbage and chemicals into them.

Source: The beginning or starting point of a river or stream. A river's source usually has clean, sparkling water.

Valley: A piece of lowland that lies between hills or mountains. Valleys often have rivers or streams running through them.

Waterfall: Running water that falls from a very high place. The sound of rushing water in a waterfall can often be heard from far away.

Index

A number that is in **boldface** type means that the page has a picture of the subject on it.

banks 6, **7**, **12**, 13, 19
barges **23**
boats **7**, **19**
bridges 6, **7**, 19, **26**, **27**, 28-**29**

cities 26, **27**
crops 20, **21**

docks 6, **7**
dragonflies 16, **17**
ducks 6, **7**

farms **21**, 26
ferryboats **25**
fish 15, 16, **19**
fishing **18-19**
flooding 20
frogs 16, **17**

garbage 15
gorges 10-**11**
grazing **20**

kingfishers 16, **17**

mills **22**, 23
motorboats 6, **7**
mud 15, 20

nets **19**

otters 16, **17**

plains 13
poles (for fishing) **18**, **19**
pollution 15

soil 9, 20
sources (of rivers and streams) 9
streams **8**, 9

valleys 10, 20, **21**
villages **25**, **26**

waterfalls 10-**11**, **20**
waterpower 23
wildlife **7**, 16-**17**